In Your Own Sweet Time

Also by Alane Rollings
Transparent Landscapes

In Your Own Sweet Time

Alane Rollings

Wesleyan University Press
Middletown, Connecticut

Some of these poems have appeared in the following periodicals: *The American Poetry Review, The Antioch Review, Carolina Quarterly, The Chicago Literary Review, The Georgia Review, Psychological Perspectives, Raccoon*, and *Sonora Review.*

I would like to express my special thanks to Courtney Campbell, Jeanne Garlington, James Belford, Edward Wolpert, and Emma and Evelyn Rollings.

All inquiries and permissions requests should be addressed to the Publisher, Wesleyan University Press, 110 Mt. Vernon Street, Middletown, Connecticut 06457

Library of Congress Cataloging-in-Publication Data

Rollings, Alane.
   In your own sweet time/ Alane Rollings.—1st ed.
     p. cm.—(Wesleyan poetry)
   ISBN 0-8195-2156-6 ISBN 0-8195-1157-9 (pbk.)
   I. Title. II. Series.
PS3568.053915 1989
811'.54—dc19   88-5746
                            CIP

Manufactured in the United States of America

This book is supported by a grant from the National Endowment for the Arts.

Frontis and part page photograph © 1987 by Jack Leigh

FIRST EDITION

Wesleyan Poetry

For Harry Evan Rollings
and Irma Lee Pittman Rollings

"and teach me how
To name the bigger light"
—SHAKESPEARE, *The Tempest*

Contents

I

Where Single Rooms Can Spring
to Life So Easily

Have you noticed how when you see two people talking
anywhere in the world, one is almost always smiling?
    Half of us are alive now; it's hard to say
what we have least of. Children come into the world
by themselves. My family began with me.
    Under my own good auspices, I took a room in the city,
gave a dollar for a smile in the street,
ten for the pressure of a hand.
I liked your stare, your air of an emporium owner.
Drinking whiskey with you in the kitchen,
I never felt a shiver of wishing to be elsewhere.
The vast melancholy of the city, that world
where single rooms could spring to life so easily,
seemed to have disappeared. You claimed as property
all you'd thought about, the fictions you had yet to overcome.
In your dreams, coats and dresses floated west
in search of tickets, of landscapes with bandstands and verandahs.
When you danced you called yourself Fernando;
your hands were as astonishing as a sublime idea.
    The way I felt would never let me be myself.
Even when I didn't know you, I was suspicious of you,
and when I knew I loved you, I suspected even more.
I knew you thought I looked like a xylophone,
even when you bombarded my windows with Indian corn,
juggled the flowerpots and rabbits of my past.
How could I stay alive with such negative emotions?
Living in the past since the day I was born,
I always remembered the wrong things—
the day my cat walked out on me,
all that milk I had in the refrigerator.
    Listening to you recall your incarnations,
it's clear you could have been anyone,
and you were. Now are you going to tell me
about your career as a comb-and-tissue player?

That happened, too. It isn't in the Guinness book of records,
but it happened. Your hands and feet explain themselves,
your wrists sloping back into your sleeves.
    I hated pink until I saw you in it. Now
I think about it all the time, your faded tights,
your improbable somersaults. It's funny
how you really seem to feel them in your heart,
the exquisite things.

    Are we so different from what we could be?
When I wish I could start over, I remember a friend
I had over there and in this room, a life
that happens only here and now. When things
seem bleak, I dream of Andalusia, a dream
I can share equally with anyone.
Are we born to be what we are?

    I suspect you now of the opening act of the heart.
I won't need to be told where to stand
when it happens to me.

Your Old Self

Last winter there wasn't any winter;
last night you dreamed about today.
Sitting here you wish for there.

When you were twenty years old, you were forty years old.
You rented an apartment, but it didn't come with sleep,
rented a piano that you played by sympathy.
At your sewing machine you whirred out a little tune,
put in some yellow thread and made a flag to wave.
When you fell in love with your world historian,
you found out where you'd be in two hundred years
and exactly what the nation thought of you.
Continually surprised by the lateness of the hour,
you couldn't see all this enthusiasm for the future:
you'd have been the same in any century.

The days never ended; they just moved ahead.
You sang "Rock of Ages" to hear a world redeemer
play his clavichord again. In matters of the heart
you were an atheist, but you returned the spoons
you'd stolen from restaurants ten years back,
wore out your clothes to donate them to charity.
In your Florida bungalow, the amethyst needle
of your Gramophone scratched out the clarinet quartet.
How proud you were of your lost causes!
Your prospects for heaven had never been better.

Time and the climate soon tell on you.
You are seen roaming your kingdom in rags
waving charts of perilous currents carefully marked.
Have all your Walter Raleighs died?
Drawbridges do not open by themselves.
You're sure that nights like these
occurred only before the World Wars.

Your banyan trees shimmer with ghosts of birds
and phantoms of dogs chase themselves
around canvas chairs and colored umbrellas,
orchids smelling of honey and roses of pears.
Your atlas moth is drying her wings
when half of Krakatoa disappears again.
You can't get over it. Maybe you've never been close enough
to a world explorer.
    Your memories dissolve into their chemical components,
but you'll never be cured of your adorations
or know what they thought of you.

    When people say of a catastrophe, "I never think of it,"
they mean that it has colored everything.
Either those days or these are not real.
Tokyo Rose is an old woman now
and Miss Liberty's copper skin is as dry as dead leaves.
You shake your cages of sleeping fever birds;
you're the same in every century.

The Age of Great Vocations

You've seen the skirts go up and down
in bread lines, soup lines, cheese lines, shanty towns.
    No one can say you aren't seeking work.
The answers come by mail at noon: No interview.
The best companies never respond; you respect them.
Some days, you don't bother to open the letters,
just tear them to bits and go out for a walk.
    It's a small fraud by the world's standard:
you can't do things like ask for directions,
so you call yourself an adventure-collector.
Failure's a field with real opportunities
for a girl with a pile of business magazines
which she will probably have to burn for heat.
Your luck will get either worse or better.
    The world is really none of your business;
it doesn't give you a living.

    Someone calls your bluff, asks for references.
You read up on yourself in the library.
With lies, you can double your existence.
    In an endless dream of introductory letters,
the applicants sit in all their best clothes,
their ages against them, their loneliness
repeated many times. The managers walk around, choosing.
You say you've done singing telegrams and balloon bouquets
(you've done strip-o-grams, sold flowers at traffic lights).
You're a cake decorator, you've been to zoo school
(you're a weeper-at-weddings, you eat cat food).
Welcome to the world of captivity.
    You were calm yesterday, and today you're thinking,
"In the days when I was calm." You'd like
to talk about your sex life. Singing your salesman's song,
you wave your thirteen letters "To Whom It May Concern,"
every one a masterpiece.
Fooling a man is a full-time job.

You've had a good day? You've found something?
The world needs you right away.
    The loneliness repeats itself.
You chart the progress of your fellow novices
who stand around as astonished as slaves
delivered in a day. They aren't moving up,
but they're saying "You bet."
They call the boss The Enemy.

    Whatever makes every beginning a sad one
suggests that somewhere there is something else for you.
Your boss is a terrorist; you like him.
Reading the impressions on his note pad,
you can't help certain hopes.
    Sitting in the switchboard glow,
connected by the movements of your hands and arms,
you're a shaky presence among solid things.
You don't get a glimpse of his heart of gold,
but you hear things he'd never tell anyone:
he spent his youth dreaming of being a thief;
he is where others ought to be;
people should be ashamed of their luck and proud of their trouble.

    At noon you sneak out and eat a stale moon pie
from a filling-station jar. You take gloves to the tramps
who stand around trash-can fires thanking God
they aren't tramps. You shake their hands.
    The job is impossible, but the enemy,
meaning your heart, is calm.
That typewriter has not got his eyes or arms:
if you accept its offer, it won't embrace you, yet it offers
itself more than he does. It won't mind
if you fall asleep in a rush at your desk
repeating to yourself, "I am asleep," or that

you can't tell in this atmosphere
the difference between sweat and tears.

You know what all the world knows: time was invented
so workdays could come to a close.
The women on the electric train
shift their weight in the direction of the men.
The men stare off, every one for himself,
every departure a sad one.
You're not the same person they regarded impatiently
over the pencil sharpener: you've escaped.
You have to lean against the window frame and laugh.
Cherishing bits of evidence of how strange you are,
you pass through glowing rectangles of town and country.
You think of knights, town criers, jesters.
You can see the world in the last light
laid out like a checkerboard, and you can live.
So you're an agent, adjuster, accommodator
with a wish to take the movements of your arms elsewhere.

Have faith in your doubts.
Your vocation is to feel
less despair about despair.

You'll be there until you leave.

Falling as a Mode of Travel

Again you hand yourself over to the sky.
Beneath you lie the streets with which your story
intertwines. There's a common sorrow there,
and in the air, everything seems to be saying good-bye.
    Once Mississippi was the capital of Jackson,
and Jackson was the only country in the world.
Your tenderness was there, and your despair.
Now all you want from it is distance.
From the Arctic Circle to the Tropic of Capricorn,
why consent to not be everywhere?

    From the sky you see things differently:
Malaya is a crocodile's head poking down into the China Sea,
and the Great Wall a dragon that couldn't keep
the secret of silk to itself. Traveling makes
a map in your mind: the feathers
which stand for mountains are your pillow; you tangle your feet
among gold threads of roads. Those standard watercolors,
browns for mountains, blues for lakes, you count
among your belongings, your life's attempts to be true.
    If memory is the same in every country,
where will you forget someone who has forgotten you?

    Half the world lost in sleep,
you reach Libreville longing for Greece,
reading in lobbies "Cairo by Car," "Nairobi by Night."
    Through continuums of light and cool
you retrace in Africa your heart-shaped path
through South America. Everyone says, "I'm a stranger here,
too." The air in Cotonou is just like Jackson's.
The Book-of-the-Month Club will never find you.

    From Paris to Prague, the faster you travel
the more lightlike you become, in and out

of enigmatic cities leading double lives.
You know them like your heart; you'll never
know them. They go the way of your dreams.
    There you are at the Rock of Gibraltar!
There you are at the Cape of Good Hope!
Buffeted by sunlight, you want to be
where you're going.
    If time is different from place to place,
won't you be younger when you get to London?

    Once he stood before your window,
and his body covered half of Jackson.
Every place has its legends; people point on maps
to mythical lakes, popular fantasies for origins of rivers.
Now you rush from light to light; you want to be
where you've been.
    There will never be another Byzantium, and the staircases
the Japanese built over mountains
have gone the way of the Chinamen who followed scents
to India, where sandalwood waited in caves of lions.

    The beautiful blanks on ancient maps have been filled in
with Antarctica, Australia. They call these mountains
Breasts of Shiva; Isola Bella floats in the sea like a body
in a gaze. Why will you never want to be
where you are?
Roads of water, iron, emptiness—
falling is your main mode of travel through the universe.
    In the deepening suspense, shift of trades, switch of poles,
where exactly is Jackson? Is there such a place as home?
Or only these long journeys made for longing,
the only thing you really own,
the meridians and tropics of the body,
its temperate zones?

Scenes of Earthly Suffering

The terrible thing that's happening is your heartbeat.
When your temperature reaches a hundred and one
you begin to leave instructions:
what's to be done with the boxes of dried umbilical cords
of the children, the snapdragons altogether capable of pain.
　　　You're an emergency only to yourself;
he's probably off making his grand rounds,
brushing another transparent face with his eyelashes.

　　　There were times in the past when your chances were
　　　　　　less than half.
In the empty auditorium of your sickroom,
there were days you prayed that they pass, just that they pass.
You drift back into the luminous world of fever
not really aware of who lifts your head to the spoon
or holds a cold sponge to your forehead.
　　　You sleep for a fraction of a second, and a fragment
of your childhood reappears. It hasn't been very useful
to grow older. Why is it
they call time the healer? He takes your hands full of fears
and returns them empty.

　　　Without his assistance you'd have to get back into bed
on your hands and knees. The trees flow together and so do
　　　　　　the streets.
He helps you back to your crumbs and pillows;
you look up at him with your milk moustache,
stop yourself with difficulty from asking him
to come and be your prisoner as you are his.
He says, "I want to see your tongue."
　　　Mistakes race through you like colored chemicals:
he's a shaman muttering incantations, kneading gemstones
to release the poison from your veins. He sits there
hopelessly holding an idiotic candle; it cramps your feet

to see him like this. He rubs your pain
to see if it works; it hurts the most
wherever he touched you last.
        Then, as someone after a nap shakes off a dream,
you look in his eyes ringed with suffering
and regarding your disasters as his own.
It's not to kiss you that his mouth is hard.
He says you can stand up again.

He has a hold on the best of human knowledge
so he drives around in a Pontiac 'til dawn.
Holy men seek suffering to intensify emotion;
he makes his sandman's rounds then prays for the night to pass,
just to pass. He used to be younger.
        There's a level of pain that buys anyone.
In embarrassment for having a body and flesh,
he wishes he could talk from the floor, crawling around.

        If he doesn't come soon they'll find you
crawling toward the emergency room. You'll need curare,
quinine, cocaine; drugs to slip out of buttons
and pour out of sleeves. He says you'll live to be ninety-three,
writes it down for your bad nights. Your pain
goes to sleep in your hand. You want to tell him
he's the man you've been encountering continually.

        The stars tilt dangerously; you're weak
and the pattern of the quilt is imprinted on your face.
He's probably at the airport waiting for a liver
to arrive in a cooler from Pittsburgh.
There's always something the matter with someone. You need
to ride in his car.
        Mysterious ailments have their purposes;
the person you're being annealed into will be more durable.

He's probably studying acupuncture, moxybustion,
and you're calm, you're touched, you're cured.
The moon has also been up all night.
    You never want to let it go—
the thrill of that continual good-bye,
the way it hurts when he shows you how
to die more slowly than you might otherwise.

for H.R., R.R., I.H., and E.W.

All the Saints Were Losers

I'm about to lay myself open to many reproaches
but how can I help it?
My prayers were all answered
with the word "No."
    The fathers told me solitude was the way to saintliness.
I copied the Bible for three hours every Friday
while saints' lives burned red and purple in the windows.
Solitude made temptation even greater.
I prayed, "Could you make room for another angel?"
Looking straight up into heaven, I could almost hear them say,
"If she comes here, we'll leave."
    I knew which mountain I would move to me.
The holy man who stroked my head and said, "Never trust
what can be seen, heard, touched." In crimson and gold
and the paper tail I'd pinned on him,
he entered my heart forever, but never warned me
about false suns, false moons, false stars.
They went on shining.

    I tried to love everyone equally, as saints do,
carved the word "desire" on my arm, wiped the cuts
with a towel soaked in wine.
    I resent preaching to myself
about eternal situations. My hands complain
when they have no one to hold. I love only you.
I count myself to sleep saying, "You. You. You."
Is this any way for a martyr to behave?
    I can stand to be tortured, but I'm not young anymore.
Here's this pillow of flesh above my heart,
a sacrifice to one whose virtue I would share.
There you are on the floor asking for "Anything, God, anything."
In the low voice of persuasion, melancholy says,
"You can't fight time with anything but beauty."
    I read my wrongs: vanity, greed, pride,
that nightly ascension of desire which knows

that nothing will be gained but further isolation.
I could change. I could change. But will I?
When will I? Could you stop praying for just a minute?

God, I hate to ask you for something like this,
but things get less explicable
though the sun shines on them night and day.
It makes it hard to get undressed
when I keep seeing the face of my judge,
his lips in my hair. Why is he laughing?
I need a little miracle,
a reward for myself just as I am.
All the saints went crazy
watching angels arrange themselves on diagonal beams of light.
The fathers, driven by devils
clothed only in blazing hair, see so well
they can do nothing else. They cheat with words; they never meant
anything they meant. They have some bad qualities too.

You think I only think about men,
am better or worse depending on them.
You ask why I still make confessions that put me in a bad light.
Well these emotions overflow in me because of you.
You cuddled me under the covers, called me "Angel,"
the usual trick.
I'm hoping to learn from your life, from the lives
of all those who moaned in their dreams.
Tell me about the history of redemption, the Eternal Feminine.
This woman who has declared her independence,
whom I have been forced to make my ally,
who is fond of casting spells and going under them,
who consists of errors and efforts,
is storming the gates of heaven with ideal constructions.
She's my consolation and may become my faith.

16

You think I'm saying these things for you,
but I want to know them for myself.
Everyone loves something other than somebody else.

Jesus, I know almost nothing about you!
Only the disintegrating stars on robes of saints,
the powdery remains of angels' haloes.
All the physical systems of the universe
operate on uncertainty principles. I look for signs;
sometimes I get them: transfigurations taking place
in imitation of great faith.

Last night I prayed.

Has anyone ever been harmed that way?

What makes a morning glory want to bloom?

Unfold your wings.
I'm not going to lose you until I have to.

Ideal Forms

"All other affections need a past. Love creates one with enchantment,
is a luminous point which takes complete possession of time."
—BENJAMIN CONSTANT

I have lived eleven thousand days.
I have been an addict and a slave.
Half my life I tried to leave my life behind me,
the other half I tried to get it back.

No sooner had I seen your face
than I supplied an age,
fit you into my chronology.
In size you were halfway between an atom and the sun.
Living among astronomical conceptions,
you surveyed the skyline with the instruments of angels
as if the mathematical theorems that operate great galaxies
could be experienced in music.
You saw the path advancing toward perfection;
why be an exception to that splendid rule?

Every time I dreamt of parallelograms,
I felt the future was already formed in me.
That blood that had issued from me painfully
had foreseen everything about your body.
You proposed desire as wisdom,
like ether that exists when you believe in it.
Studying Greek statuary with a compass,
I knew what made reality reality:
the ideal way your back squared off
and ran down to the rest of you.

The day I understood the integral,
I knew that language lacked a million words
and why lovers love infinity.
If I could understand the despair in an adagio,
life would be a problem in higher mathematics.
Movements of my arms around your torso
would make you my certainty as I was yours.

I redesign my keyboard, forge hexameters,
shape pendulums from bits of thread and little balls of clay.
Why not transform gravity to music,
faith to matter, everything into everything else
in any order whatsoever?
If I could describe our life together,
I'd have no need of another.

The Love Among Time, Space, and Sleep

Someone said everyone has the same secrets.
But here where everything seems equidistant, infinitely near
            and inaccessible,
and we have mixed desires to die now and to live forever,
we have our doubts. Are we glad we went to school? Are we happy
to be definitely human, eating and drinking symbols
in the silence where our secrets germinate?
Time has seen us, day after day: we walk and we fall
and we walk and fall and we fall and fall and fall.
We are the space we displace, the weight before we fall.
        Eventually our bodies learn the rules of dignity:
90°, no stumbling, no stuttering, no decisions in favor of extremes.
If the laws would forget us, our lives would be ours
for the taking,
so we say, our voices filled with beautiful constructions.
I'd be buried on Mars, just to be up there.
But somebody draws the line, and even the air-bound faces
of dancers and acrobats are not the faces of flight;
their eyes are not the eyes of flight, blank and bright
and innocent as sculpture. They are only human
and the air is thick with mysteries that will not move on,
flung with wishes and inhibitions that will not move on.
        Under the same sheets, the same spell,
we sleep in shifts, aware of the risks we are taking,
and read each other's dreams in movements of mouths and eyelids:
        I see you have been raking rocks all day and have not heard
of gravity. A wind flips into your sleeves
and children in nearby wheatfields cry, "The man has wings!"
Your body stretches like a figurehead
and people begin to compare you with poplar trees and upward
            cataracts;
you rest and float in the air and sometimes fall in love
with things—you bring me dozens of clay dolls from Mesopotamia
and the fresh bones of a pterodactyl from North Dakota

and when your silver emissaries summon you
I understand your need to shout at them.
Surely the horizon is a line to cross over and over,
and everyone the world over is surely dreaming
of the evolution of wings out of fins, paws, feet.
   In the meantime sleep has seen me
wrapped in a gray-blue cloud which unwinds and does not own
      up to me.
I fall and you fall and we fall and we see
what a wish it was to be laid out like mist
above the world that brought us up. So we see.
So it goes. We have fallen awake
in the adept and experienced arms of time
which alone owns the sky and the gates of space.
We've been a long time coming back to earth.

We are thinking of building a roof again,
perhaps putting our doors back on their hinges.
So we say.
(May we keep falling as long as we live . . .

Terra Incognita

If only we were born old and grew younger—

On the street you're at the mercy of the centuries
that precede you; you're on the open sea.
Everything acts mysteriously upon you:
a new body appears on your horizon;
its orbit in some imperturbable way affects your own.
You go for advice to thunderclouds,
carry garnets to discharge the disquiet in your body.
Why not sling ideas around? Disorder has its charm.
(If only you chose the people that you loved.)
        Things are visible, but as if they do not quite
believe in themselves. Chrysanthemums blossom
in the shape of bodies, and a hand,
a burning cogwheel of fingers, moves upward
toward a mouth, shooting sparks like electricity.

What order do you want to give nature now?
There are things that make you think the earth
is capable of happiness; others merely seem to be themselves:
comets jaywalking across the paths of planets,
the huge heavy mechanism of your heart.
        If only there were ships waiting for you
at the end of every street—
But your ocean has moved inward; your astronomers
are within you, too. They tell you space is full of fire,
go through what's clear, and conclude it's the mysterious
that's beautiful. One moment your heart is a rock,
the next a gemstone, climbing sideways in the sky.

There was a time when nothing had been done before.
Ruled by the past as if it were the universe,
you think of days when theories were proven
within themselves. Poppies blossomed in veins,

and bodies were random daydreams that could be had again,
whenever, as mimosa spoke to sugar maple.
    Where do you find time to imagine these things?
What happened to them? Did they shimmer away
like the sad little ghosts inside you
who are given to dropping things? Everything happens,
everything. Desire bleeds in your mouth,
burns your lips like the live coal of a prophet.

    Your heart hangs in the garden, and you offer
in atonement every generous moment of your life.
Every afternoon you traipse about; the logic of the clouds
doesn't work on your nerves.
    When asked what you've thought of
to rescue your future, if only you can answer
that lost processes are less beautiful than electricity
or trade the hands of a conjurer
for the mandrake clusters of Solomon's Song
that lift you on the slow wings of their history
and take you places you could never go alone.

Elementary

How do you live? Do you imagine your life
before it happens? When I match memories with you,
I conclude we're both impossible.
    I want to go over the evidence that you are here with me.
I'll take a compass and trace a circle around us,
then compute the degree of inclination
of your feet while you are sleeping,
dreaming yourself to what you could have been.
    You must be someone. Should I trust the memory
of your uncle? You emit one two-thousandth volt,
make up your mind on water and carbon molecules.
You have a present of zero duration, two pasts
and two futures; one of each is happy.
To you, memories are electrical phenomena
and the future is whatever happens next.
You're always paying back those loaned minerals that you are;
you're always thinking of that word "happiness."

    Your sleeping face makes up for many things.
I remember meals I made for you,
and in my mind, make them again, more tenderly.
The double X chromosomes of my chemistry,
abloom and ablaze like lemon trees deceived by streetlights
into their complicated metamorphoses,
convince me there are moments when hands and mouths
don't lie. The moon, the lamp, your tilted face
are one star diminishing in radius, heavy elements
trapped in its heart.
    I think I might find something in that face
that would allow me to surpass myself.
Ovulating to the forty-watt full moon,
desire makes me open a jar as I will remember having opened it,
makes orchids smell like female bees,
asks simple questions: "Don't you know a butterfly

when you see one?" I'm drawn toward your flesh
when it denies itself to me, like the rest of what is mine.

    In your dreams you're too tall to stand in a room with me.
You burst through walls and stroll through town like a giant,
caress the landscape, hold the present
like a diamond in your giant hand, tell flowers
charmed into blooming too soon, "You fools! There will be
none of you left for summer!" You have proof
only of yourself, and if you want to talk about the table,
you have to start with the creation of the universe.
Everything reminds you of something else and nothing
of itself: the butterfly simulates a flower that simulates
a bird. You sum up my studies in science.
    I sit here twirling a cup to fill up time,
feeling with neither the iron of my blood nor the skin
of my face the race and spin. Lithium springs bubble up
for the sufferers of mania, and a caterpillar
goes through all the tests and concludes that it's a caterpillar.
It's not a matter of brains, but confidence.

    The moon hovers over the town, a measure of its longing,
and you turn again into the person who belongs to me.
I thought we were often unhappy; now it seems
that misery was just an aspect of our happiness.
We rotate with respect to one another; in mid-embrace
I realize you are looking at the table, I am thinking of a jar.
    In this room where everything testifies to our presence,
I'm reassured by the sway of the moon over water.
What holds is held, and everything
is building up to something else:
solutions, explanations,
the great dream words "now" and "somehow"—
elements the earth never gave birth to.

812-0147

Sweet Luck

Some people won't be disappointed.

You wanted to earn each turn of fate.
Standing at the table in your beige summer suit,
you stirred your summer drink and met your failures.
Wondering why you were unhappy,
you took up magic, gambling, and a hundred ways
to give yourself away—the blush, the sudden
laughter. You lost the game,
the car, the house, the curtains
sucked in by the shutters.

There's decidedly no reason why things go wrong.
100,000 Peruvians in the streets
after an earthquake, and the Abyssinian high plateau
turns to dust, the people eat their seed corn, blow away.
Why did your mother's other children come into life dead?
Alone in your shop of silver wheels,
you shake hands with yourself, proud to be
as real as anything. You want to be of use to orphans.
You say to me, "Jump on my stomach.
See what an iron man I am!"

The life we were suspected of we never lived.
I had an ice-cream cone, you had a sandwich; you lived to lose
on the fruit machines. Then there were
100,000 starving people leaning without resentment
against a sheep-pen wall. You were who they wanted to be.
You expected to be led to caves
where dwarves played with diamonds, to castles
where naked girls lay sleeping.
You got a game of rules and points and zigzags,
days when everything you had got confiscated
because you didn't use it.

It can be anything that puts you in that place—
The End. You beg yourself: "Please, Jack."
You pray for magic. You recognize your wishes
by improbability.
    Busloads of bingo players
wind around the desert—30,000 losers
trying to improve their chances with Hawaiian charms.
    In the artificial dark of billiard rooms,
you win awhile, you lose, you go on losing.
I gather up my little strength and offer it like money.
    Everybody has a house that leaves him
in a hurricane, and there are dust children,
dust-of-life, with eyes ashamed of opening.

    If you only knew how beleaguered I feel in this castle,
mistress of a palace disappearing into winter.
I could desire something.
I see your legs through your dark trousers;
they don't look confused to me. Turn right for the castle.
    But I've got to warn you about these fantasies.
There are 431 steps to the Temple of 10,000 Buddhas
and 100,000 luck strips at the Temple of Wang K'ai Su.
If you're smart you won't trust them.

    When I lie with you and everything sways,
you turn away in your intractable dream
of living at all times and as almost everyone.
I stroke you and your pulse accelerates. The race is on.
    If only you could know you'd last a lifetime,
that one day the gems, the wheels, the gate
would swing into your waiting arms—
    Dream on, Jack. You can tell the story now,
knowing more or less how it turns out.

A History of Diminishing Distance

(on the return of Halley's Comet)

If a bright light flashes across the sky,
it's not a comet. Far above the atmosphere,
they do change their attitudes, but slowly.
The terrors of the neighborhood, they cruise by, breaking
rules. We have to watch them closely.

No one has seen you lately. What have you been doing
with your hazardous existence? You said you had
been kidnapped when you missed my train; you said
your grandmother died when you didn't meet me at the airport;
she died again when you didn't show up for supper.
You had an interesting conception of the marvelous.

While sailors gambled their lives on the mathematics
of a man from Alexandria, Arabs left their algebra and harems
to record the visits of the great Guest Stars—
omens sent by gods to the emperors of China, Greece, and Rome.
We're still stationed at our tripods
awaiting a phenomenon so complete in beauty
we can hardly hope for sense.

You too can be beheld as a distant object. You'll
grow old but that's not what you make me think about.
Do you remember how we met? I arranged myself
so that our bodies were parallel, whirling
about the common field of ourselves.
I still can't believe that anything is accidental.
I think of the future the way I did at seventeen:
we said "Good-bye forever" every day,
then ran back, said it again.

Woven into the Bayeux tapestry and painted by Giotto,
the comet sailed by like a century: brightening, brightening,

then dimming, disappearing. While Tycho in his fancy robes
saw nothing but perfection in the heavens, Halley set out
to chart the southern stars.

After I found out time was moving,
I got the feeling it was speeding up. I foresaw myself
vanish in the middle of the street. I looked for you
everywhere. Were you deciding always to be alone?
You spun on your heel, said, "Give me time
forever," then turned back and held the clock
against your cheek, the polished wood cool against your skin.
We took a nap together. I don't remember it,
I was asleep. Thank God I'll never be twenty again.

While Messier hunted comets from a Paris tower
cowboys sold comet pills, paid off their mortgages.
Some said comets caused the Flood, others outbreaks
of sanity and love. (Expect strange things, they'll happen.)
Some won cash prizes, others died of fear.
Why should we be afraid of our pasts?
We can see each other there.

You came back from darkness glad for everything—
the lit-up house, the dress I wore, your suitcase full of junk.
There you were, your breath on me. You said
you were as constant as the speed of light.
How on earth did we spend our best days
if fifteen years alert for the miraculous
hasn't been enough for me to understand you?
You, of all people, getting caught like this!
You'll go through a lot more still before you're done
with this odd joke. I'll probably find you in a deck chair,
an invalid, your unperturbed gaze unfixed by the soft air.

What will it be? Nothing, just old age.
You don't think about it, then suddenly it's on its own way.

So let the years pass. Come to today.
You're always late. The sun's done what it's famous for;
the pyrotechnical display's about to start. The bridge
lights up, the airstrip, streetlights, headlights, houselights.
The stars thank their stars they're stars. They paint the sky
with fire. I close one eye and suddenly
remember forty things about you. To think I might
have gone on drawing the shades all my life.

The night assistant, given the celestial coordinates
of target galaxies, collects light in little glass plates,
establishing over the long night the expansion of the universe,
and an old Spinozan skeptic, confused by flashing lights
and stopwatches, sees stars and imaginary cars
spinning and vanishing in the whirlwind he has raised.
What's the idea? There isn't any,
only fragile mechanisms of before and after.

There you are.
There's always something drawing you apart
from everything. It isn't time. You must say life.

As if we were the dreams of gods and they were ours
the comet comes again, a little fainter. You compose
from flashes images of years. We are
our own dreams. You must say life.

II

The Light of Bright Interiors

It's dangerous to stay in a place where you've been very happy.
  My theme is the daily gentleness between two people: some
      sunlight
intercepted by a wooden fence, a house full of books
about the lives being lived inside.

  In the first weeks it is decided
that she will be untamable. He'll shelter her
against the harm he'll do her. She'll have the privilege of
      being loved
a little less. The common objects will be liberated by a white
      erotic light
from their ugliness. He'll hug her, toss her, catch her,
kiss her, whose molecules are his, who laughs
because he laughs.
  Every day she learns things she should have known for years.
She sees him seeing everything and wants him never to leave
because she never wants to go anywhere herself.
  They live in the present tense, like saints.
Fleshed in their imaginary versions of themselves, they sleep
as though no passions and torments had ever raced through
      their veins
and dream to perfection the same things again and again.

  They were already sick of the picture they made,
the walls he built out of nothing at all,
the sleep he slept only out of nostalgia for his dreams.
Her loyalty was atonement, her endless troubles
the necessity of his existence. They pitied things
they hadn't bothered to bring to life—sparkling paperweights,
clothes on the line, the three sides in the dark of both of them.
  Thirty years earlier, birds had flown through the place;
the cottage had raised its four roofless walls to the sky.
The contractors hadn't been paid.

So days go by and nights go, too.
Years are lost and she must account for them somehow;
she doesn't want to have to reconstruct herself again.
She knows what she did the same day last year
and the year before that.
Saving her cents-off coupons, she's a star customer.
She knows also how everything watches; wallpaper
has a better memory than she.
At night he becomes a streak of light;
she'll probably understand him unexpectedly after he disappears.

She throws out incidental things—sweaters and pillows
soft, desired, forgotten. What on earth is she doing here?
She wants to go live in a tree,
hauling things up on a rope.

The shutters keep swinging, the light reflecting
from well-waxed floors, recollections shimmering
near a surface. There is evidence that she exists
and is unusual, just because they live together here,
in listening distance, in the light of this bright interior.

What is the difference in color between a shadow of an apricot
and one of a plum? In the strange light cast by her confusion
the house becomes a museum of all that was wished for and forgotten
and that difference in tint, the problem life hinges on.

Dusting her treasures, she fills with feeling
as a room with light, prepared, unready,
uncertain of what is, relatively, the happiest fate.
The wings of an airplane tilt upward, setting the houses
below on edge. In this one, two people tell the same story
in the same room, his way and hers. They don't think
the universe knows anything about them.

There's nothing about this life they could have imagined.
Not one thing.

Not this constant harmony of the most excessive colors,
not the same colors again and again.

  I never see myself in any other future
but trying once more for our happiness
on that street one hundred yards long.
There's a garden alive with chameleons
and fireflies changing the code of their flashes.
Light grows at the edges and corners of the windows:
that's your nightshirt flickering through the gloom,
your slippers flapping.
The street has returned you home in a burst of yellow light,
a primary-colored intensity of longing
for more time, more air, more light, a month in the mountains,
a mystery softened by familiarity.
  There's your light going on again.
Here's the old ache that makes beauty what it is,
the same beauty again and again.
When you sit in the sun, you don't need proof of it.

for Dick

Emma S. and the Pearls of Beatrice d'Este

It is the pearls about da Vinci's portrait
of Beatrice d'Este, the luminous constellation of her pearls,
around her head, collecting in a wave
upon her neck, about her breasts, each a new
transparency into this lady, as if to show
the rows of shade in her complexion and the sky
as they appeared from day to day.
The pearl for instance in the cleft betrays
the way that water has arranged a meeting
between trees and clouds, embracing them together.
This pearl contains a drop of lace, and that of flesh—
each view, bit of her dew, vaporous as a new breath.

Emma S.—in an old photo with idyllic unconvincing
background, in white lace and her feathered hat,
that back that never touched a chair's,
her waves of hair a frame around her face.
My grandmother, who got up early from our cave of breath
to give herself enough time to get dressed. I watched her
fix upon her head that rope of her own hair
saved strand by strand, and knew that somewhere
in her was my father's mother, further still a maiden name.
It is the portrait's Emma S., the bright interior,
that I have left. She who felt naked without her necklaces
yet was so sure of heaven. I have re-dressed her
in her frailties, her vanities, her memories
and made my own translucencies—certain that the picture holds
beneath her dress the crinolines, the camisole,
the breasts. Why separate these things, these girls?
There is a beauty that becomes them both
and draws them close.

The Fate of Tenderness

Some love the word "love" more than others.

Again and again he appeared on the edge of your life
in his waterproof coat, a man who was kinder
without his clothes on. (Some just watch the transit
of tenderness in themselves and do nothing about it.)
You could see everyone else's face in your mind
except his. A long-lost type, who had walked
into your life and become your life in a city minute.

As young girls do who work upon themselves with color,
swaying before their mirrors on slender ankles,
you beseeched your life to begin.
To imagine his face, you had to start
with the razor cuts on his chin.
The dearest things about him were the simplest—
the question mark of his torso, curved at the shoulders,
straight at the hips.
In your breasts you were a mother already;
you'd suckled kittens, dug up their graves in grief.

To some, a *pas de deux* is always a love story;
to others, music and dance are nothing but music and dance.
But this beauty-emotion and those love-shocks
over the kittens' silken tails, sandpaper tongues—
aren't they one and the same?

As baby geese follow whatever moves, a girl
goes to sleep in midsummer, wakes,
and falls in love with the first living creature she sees,
strokes his paws and stares for an hour, kisses his horn.
There's a world-wide longing—war-born babies
deposited in cradles revolving in darkness at monastery gates,
couples closing doors for the torture of the lonely,

and the torn-off separate beauties of the body,
a woman's arms detached from her shoulders,
forever unclasping her pearls.

He showed up in camouflage colors.
Holding your constancy between your breasts
you said, "You've undressed everyone else,
now undress me." You tended his bruises of musical origin
with your mouth, noticed how he closed you, opened you.
Your devotion got on his nerves.
He found his trousers under the floorboard.
When you tried to imagine him after that,
all you could see were disconnected eyebrows.
So much tenderness
transformed to sadness, lost, misused, extravagantly spent—
family men killing their families,
children making love and driven mad in the dark.
In your breasts he left you
dirty little girls who will never be women,
women who will never be mothers.

Some women never complain about how heavy men are.
Some lovers always call each other
"Baby."
You don't need to see him
to see him.
The silver domes of monasteries
float above the forest
where a lioness with a crushed jaw
has left her cubs to her sister.
In the obliquity of sunshine,
you make your pact with solitude
and love those who
have less love than you.

Everyone Looks at the Sky

Everyone you know anything about lived here,
decked out for the latest occasions
scheduled to take place off some latitude,
some longitude. Everyone looks at the sky, hangs out
of windows to see whatever goes on and on
and on. Everyone knows why prisoners love the moon.

You left the scene with a temple concealed in your flesh
the way an ordinary thief would swallow a jewel.
Now you've begun to notice the beauty of the landscape
you're escaping over. Wild animals return to remembered beauty;
your treachery is the same as the stars', the cedars'.
Are you all man? I bite into you out of sheer love
and whisper with the eagerness of hunger, "Do I mean
something to you?" Yes, you are a man.
I remember when you first descended
from the branches with your ten million brain cells.
Are you comfortable with your body yet? News of pain
will travel to your brain in advance of pain,
to prepare you for it. But no matter how real
your grief is, it won't have official approval.

Ask. But what are you going to ask for?
An end to your search for comfort, for the sweetness
of another human form? (I don't need light
to think of you.) Do you think
that because you baptize the stars with your stares
that it's you who populated heaven
with bears, dogs, and archers?
Bound to the astrolabe, the compass,
you carry your orphanage around with you,
set up prisons wherever you go.
You count your cosmic rays, but prowling in the dark
on unknown grounds, you can't follow them, they can't follow
themselves.

Sneezing in the sun
with the gravity which makes you say,
"But we must *think*—"
you waver between diamond mines and the missionary church.
Can you blame the pagans who kick their gods
when they won't hear their prayers? Apollo,
are you there? God of yellow daisies, save us
from sweat and insects.

Whenever I need to reconstitute a male body,
I pretend I am nibbling on your gingerbread heart.
Your eyes are still there and I'm still there behind them
and the Mediterranean speaks from your lips.
Einstein waved away the cosmic uncertainties
that flowed from his own majestic equation;
as governor, you would have enough power to blow your nose.
You were born with an open wound:
the singing mouth of a figurehead exposed on some shore
of paradisiac nakedness and staring cockatoos.
You look at the sky a true navigator
charting a course as immaculate as a swan's,
and wondering if God isn't just another lonely old Jew.
You're as solid as light and as obstinate.

Those Slow Confusions of Our Pasts

Nothing I confide to myself surprises me now.
I have decided to go back over my shabbiest memories,
those slow confusions of our pasts.
A late child, low in vitality, with birdlike bones,
born too soon to see more of the universe
than photographs of Jupiter, its nine moons,
that Voyager was sending back as it flew on
to Saturn, bearing our greetings in sixty languages.
We were a small way station, womanless and lawless,
an island with a lighthouse, a lighthouse with an island.
By trade, you were a trader—pursuing wakes of ghost ships,
describing Venice to the weightless child sprawled over you,
half dreaming the half-covered dreams of public travelers.

In fickle and unfavorable winds, landbound,
you waved the light away and taught me Homer, Gulliver, and Crusoe
in sentences that never dreamed of being finished.
This was history. You sat behind your desk and wrote
about your daughter, who grew up. Passing you on the stairs,
my barely female body stuck to the wall.
You asked me once if everything was clear.
Thank heaven you made no further effort to communicate;
I had only my reservations, and even less assurance in the evenings.
I burned my moon books, offered up some minor sacrifices,
and prayed for medicine to tell me who I was.
Coal-eyes and diamond-brained, you called me,
your teenaged missile.
The outermost moons of Jupiter had never been brighter.
I could see their frozen tidal waves and waterquakes;
we were on the verge of some new chemistry,
another physics past interpretation.

"Am I sweet?" I wondered.
A fit mother for my murdered mysteries?
I wanted to waltz out of your life like a leaf.
I ran to meet the thieves who came each month like relatives,
the sad marines who called for me with tattooed hands,
tossed their gleaming wrenches to the moon
and rigged their boats again.
    My first blind date was the only one
who didn't leave me jilted.
With an empty purse and not even a single lipstick,
and only a touch of the bird about me,
I loved you best and left,
half-dreaming, but in Homer's hands.

Search, Rescue, Search

I met him yesterday. He was my best friend.
(I have always been mistaken about the objects of my desire.)

On a day too calm to be called hopeless,
I was taken in by the strangeness of things.
The everyday life I longed for
showed not the slightest sign of beginning.
I justified myself by ranging far,
so that I could say, "I have looked everywhere."
    I went my way as far as it could take me,
driven by disbelief that I could go so far
and be no closer to my pearling grounds.
In the achingly silent air
I took my bearings from mistaken landmarks,
believing in too much and not enough.
Why did I neglect to learn the stars?
A lost mariner on a blue-green sea
dreaming up and down—
Others haven't drowned here, why do I?

On a midday without sun or hope,
my long accident of life was nearly over.
As if he'd read the messages left in the air
behind me, the water I beat and fought
for my breath, he took my face in his hands
and turned it a different way.
(My hero let me touch that pear-shaped muscle
under all those other ones.)
    As if he were the representative
of all the complex passions,
this man from the South without good times to give me
put his chest to my breasts, his mouth to my mouth,
and filled my lungs with sundust,

filled my head with the blue light
of high altitudes.
Have I ever loved what I thought I loved?

    In the summer hills, the summer heat,
I search for those three hours; I'm on my knees.
His breath that I breathed then I'm breathing still;
I still hear what I heard: "I have looked everywhere."
    Believing in too much and not enough.
I made love into a proverb, all the proverbs.
    In my memory he never touched me.

    Why do some rejoice and some despair?

Problems in Astronomy

Lately I've made some clear observations.
(Once in a while the moon makes me go logical.)
There's you and then there's the rest of the universe.

Could you live without the sun and stars,
things that are always just beyond,
that can go on and on without us
and we must be glad they will?
We've been instructed about these bodies: we are here
and they are there, and nothing
comes between us. We see them
reappearing in a thousand different attitudes
but never as they are.
And yet we say we love them.
My long close scrutiny of you
has given me no order within myself.
I count by eights to ten thousand, waiting
for your sleep to deepen. Around you
the illusion of existence extends to everything—
arms of chairs, table legs, thrown off overthings
dispersed in some mysterious scheme
that can't be casual. Your stream of visitors
has given way to one
who summarizes all those who have seen you sleep—
Dianas hurling javelins in the nowheres of your dreams.

I've been hoping for a miracle in reverse,
something to remove your magical effect.
But your face and hands remain incomparable symbols
of a strange astronomy. You take facts
out of my life. In your sublunary regions,
reality has no rights. Now and then,
when you've taken me into the light upon light of your arms,

even the sight of the sky has been
a thing of the past.

Like all my theories, you are busy
getting out of hand. Why be foreseeable?
Fifty-five crystalline spheres were enough for Aristotle,
but why let sentiment have any hold on you?
You sleep in the arms of Amazons
who are not only invisible themselves,
they make everything they touch invisible.
I see only shadows cast in moonlight
by a man multiplied by fantasy.
The interstellar space between us
is twice as empty in the night.

I don't believe the struggles of love are ever over,
but now and then my eyes do me a favor.
As Athens built a fleet from olive groves,
I plot a course. You start to kiss me;
it starts to rain. The scarlet silk
of your umbrella wheels away
like one of Atalanta's apples.
The strange thing is,
it's not the only thing that's beautiful.
I can always ache
for the disorder
of your underclothes,
but once in a while
when the moon and stars shine brilliantly
out of the dark history of our nonexistence,
I'm pleased to imagine you
drifting among your satellite galaxies
dreaming of yourself with someone else.

All's Fair

How the home front suffers!

I have nothing sensible to say to you.
"Unbearable" and your name are two words that ring in my head.
With banging doors, flying shoes,
we break the laws of love again.
What are we doing wrong?

I can't find my way about in this anger anymore.
As battles break up histories of nations,
every word we speak has come between us.
Clouds of dish-dust sparkle upward:
what we have, we fight for.
Shouts whirl down the hall
like dancers in a spell of adoration:
what we've lost, we fight for.
What else are we doing wrong?

What did you tell me to read
when I asked you during those first days to be my teacher?
War and Peace, nothing but *War and Peace*.
Because we thought that history depended
upon our gentleness in privacy,
it was all that was needed to make us lower our voices.

Aren't we a classic?
Years and years of deathless romance later,
here I am again banging a pot in the street,
my belongings parked on the sidewalk.
Our meaningful succession of exchange
broken by the way you say I was
(by you who made me what I was),
I search for my old trenches,
write curses in the dirt beneath your window.

In the blue fire of the barricades,
I can't find my way about anymore.
I want to discuss Tolstoy, but the real story
took place in our heads, improvised by passions, stratagems.
It's pointless to call on perfect harmony:
in every two, each one comes from a foreign country.
Loyalty, reoccupy my dangerous, dark heart.
I have a right to run after your car
screaming your name as a soldier wears
a miraculous text as talisman.

The point is, it all should have been more beautiful—
here it is, that last word that I have to have—
but I never knew I could love you calmly,
never knew.

Long Gone

All of the people who told you how to behave
are dead now. Most of them deserved it. You
are older than you intended to be.
The pain that's been roaming around for years
has gone to your head, a traveling show
in the outskirts of your body.
There have been fortunes in everything you've done;
it simply wasn't you who found them.
Full of futures, all you need are facts:
oxygen turns scarlet blood to purple;
plants make oceans green;
life creates the sky.
Basically, you're the same as a tree,
shoving for sunlight with astonishing slowness.
You got smarter, began to talk,
sent your prayers to the special section of heaven.
Did the dinosaurs disappear to escape the first flowers?
Only the birds are left of them. They say
you are also a danger to yourself.
Afraid your body will fail you,
you look for someone to worry you back to life.
She comes on a pony, dragging the sea behind her.
You wake up hopeful; soon you see there are still
two of you. You don't even resemble each other.
The fun's over; better go recite your male progenitors.
Only the old know enough to console you,
and your children will never have enough science.
Your words float in Lysol, but the infection
spreads. Close that window; don't you want
to remember yourself? Don't eat that; you don't know
where it's been. That isn't a maiden you see before you;
it's a vamp led astray by Ezra Pound.
They catch you alone and that's it.
They catch you together and all you can do
is exchange one look.

Once and for all you decide to stop bleeding.
You can't help but notice how improbable
facts can be. You look up the way ducks look at airplanes;
you look at strangers as if there is hope;
you do your duty of calling everything by another name.
Everything dies for itself and what are you
going to do about it? You didn't get
to write The Constitution. Console yourself with the cruelty
of science fiction, the violence of nursery rhymes.
At the drop of the loop in the cyclical process
of coming to be, your migrant nostalgias
and all your loose ends will condemn you.
Down will come baby, toppling you
before unpitying gods, sending you
to secret meetings with yourself, your father always away
and his absence always with you,
and your fiancée keeps postponing the wedding.
     Sitting between her spleen and liver,
you study her with the face of a faith healer
gazing at regeneration. Fifty-thousand pounds of pearls
will not buy you the tiniest piece of soul,
but you're reassured that it's possible
to speak of something besides yourself:
the perfect solids of Pythagoras; Wren's interiors;
Malraux on beauty. Recovering, always
recovering. Why live by faith? You have forgetfulness.
On his deathbed, dismantling his memories,
Stravinsky wrote, "Oh how I love you!" instead of his name.
Tycho Brahe, wearing his gold nose, said over and over,
"Let me not seem to have lived in vain!"
If Brahms were here, he'd cry in your arms;

he'd say, "Never before
have I heard my lullaby so well played!"
Were these men mirages? Their inspirations
seem less labored now.

You will inscribe your history in the memories of birds
a universe before the dinosaurs come back to the gardens.
Swans don't sing when they die of grief.
Long gone the days when love was all
that it had to be.

The End of the World

Mornings like this make history
out of people with faces like ours.
  You return every morning from the beyond
to a world that repeats itself.
The days repeat the sure, daily, reassuring blue,
a flag that everyone wakes and stands to.
At night you do your research on the end of the world.

  I said I wouldn't love you in a million years.
The woman who said that has a different memory;
I must have dreamt her.
On your account, she acquired a need for a future.
(She loves him—she thinks about it all day long,
can't stop kissing the top of his head. Sometimes
she has these love-attacks in her legs.)
  On your account, I knew that love made us
invent the beautiful. I measured us
against the evolution of intelligence
on a planet held in place
by the graceful, blue arms of spiral galaxies.
  You said you'd love me only if I were the only woman on earth.
When I asked you about that later, you said I'd dreamt it.
By then, I'd become the only woman on earth
who saw in your eyes her whole life, the whole world,
the stars in their mysterious positions
of ascension and decline.
  The light that raced to our eyes
brought us no news of the future;
it gave us a need to be equally tender to all,
as if we were dying, and tenderness were
the end of everything.

You wake up so the world can continue,
scramble breakneck out of your radioactive dreams
to a beautiful, daily day. You wish you were a cat or a bird

with nothing to feel history by. Sometimes your grief
follows you across the bounds of sleep; you wake up
wandering around in the snow in your tee-shirt.
     Love makes the world an emergency set to music.
Couples in every corner of the world
pour each other full of color
from every angle of the human face.
They could follow each other to the ends of the earth,
or then again, they could be atomized any minute
and flashed away as particles of light-dust.

     Desire repeats desire, and everything
that can happen must. Look how love
is also given as the motive of maniacs
who wish to decorate the sky.
     Look, this planet isn't a dandelion going to seed. It's
your story. A merry-go-round with real ponies
and swanlike boats and primary colors magically intense
and multiplied—how is it
that everyone isn't worrying over it?

     Maybe the Garden of Eden was a spaceship.
Maybe the person of two hundred thousand A.D.,
who replaces your imaginings with his own, will be
a tiny thing with fabulous kits for feet.
You'll be an antediluvian monster known by your bones.
Maybe there will be time to complete a feeling.
     Then again, five billion years could pass,
a day would come when clouds would smoke
and oceans simmer; the sky would open
and everyone look in and know
how dying feels to the sun.
They'd say, "No one's to blame. We all
did everything." Maybe that would be enough. Maybe.

We trust yesterday more than tomorrow,
love tomorrow more than today.
We'll ask the world for a repeat performance.
I don't want a gift of the last remains
of your feelings, your heart's countdown, when really
there is no end to this tenderness, these simple ordinary hopes
that justify tomorrow—the kiss good night, the kiss awake—
as if nature were planning to make an exception
and leave us here to the end of time.
A man of your mind can do anything, and it's not
the end of the world. (Bless this day.)

Irma Lee

One weekend when she came home from college
her mother was standing in the front yard
smiling, in sun and a new dress.
Before she left on Sunday,
her mother had given her the dress.
One weekend when she stayed at school
she lost her home, her father, and her mother.
When she did get home, there was only
what was left by the tornado.
She and her sister spent a morning walking through the rubble
in case there was anything to find—
anything small and solid—silverware,
a silver box of money—every woman had one.
Her mother had called her name before she died,
mistaking the woman who'd found her for my mother:
"Irma Lee—"

There were other things about that time
I have been promised to be told sometime.
Sometimes I have an image of my mother
younger, wearing a dress of mine.

In the Days Inside the Night

"Why does the mind see more clearly in sleep
than the imagination of the day?"
—LEONARDO DA VINCI

The ceiling gleams above a blue as black
as blue can be, and our hearts give out, as always.
We suffer what one does for love,
assailed while continuing to talk of other things.
  In the days inside the night, we dream of sleep.
Our solitude could not be more complete inside a mountain.
We make our way through movements of arms
as slow as those of branches.
Are we happy, thinking that we hold all ways
into our hearts again?
We move as if through pictures in a stereopticon;
everything is as contiguous as it should always be,
and the knight who opens his shoulder like a casket
and takes out a honeycomb resembles you.
Every idea is someone; everything takes shape.
  As beautiful as a row of calendar moons,
a line of miners begins dismantling a mountain.
Their helmets shine like swans,
and they are unattached to our chronology.
They don't know what leads to what, and of course they're happy.
Whose memories are these
that grow like quartz flowers out of prehistoric paintings?
What place is this, so much more magnanimous
than anyone we know?
  Dreams make their own facts, as always,
as if we'd spent our lives inside a crystal
composed of a hundred other crystals.
When did we forget our multiplication tables?
What was it about each other that we loved?

  Anyone can find out the amount of metal in the sun,
but no one knows what happens
to the three fourths of our lives that are absolutely missing.
We sleep as always, and the dust of memory
assumes the shape of towns

56

whose streets are being torn up silently,
leaving old women with their silver walkers
to topple into the earth with the infinite speed of stillness.
Will we ever put anything back where it belongs?
    Bound hands and feet and delivered to our pasts,
we are offered diamonds for a simple hunger,
promised tiers of choirs when we've only missed one person.
There are mother lodes of antimony, molybdenum, and zinc
as beautiful as passages of Theocritus.
Where are our true fields of energy?
    Down our dreamlines,
past pylons, flights of steps, and waterfalls,
isn't there one zone of purity and happiness
from which we aren't excluded,
and where there is an always?

In Your Own Sweet Time

To bear your life you need accompaniment.
You apply for a license, buy crystals, and listen through the skip.
The world comes through in staccato bursts, bouncing
off the ionosphere. You can pick up Paris and WXRT,
Yo-Yo Ma and The Jefferson Starship.

In the soft light of an auditorium
beyond which it snows and grows dark,
the orchestra waits for the audience to stop arguing.
The audience waits for the music. A theme
of long separation begins. The audience makes up and holds hands.

In the Arctic Ocean, a humpback whale picks up a song
on the note he'd dropped it on a month ago.
In the auditorium, a thousand people
give themselves to symmetry. Scenarios of night and day
solemnly unroll. I hadn't heard that piece
since I had to listen to you play; I listened
the whole way through the way I never would to you,
slamming away at your piano on the sun porch
as though you were on stage. When you got stuck on the bells
the termites beat their heads on the floor,
flinging themselves into space.
A thousand people applaud. I put my heart
into the hand you hold. A Japanese woman
kisses her violoncello, a fish clicks his teeth
to the tympani of a school of mollusks, and a thrush
stops in mid-song and begins again, dissatisfied.
When I told you what I'd been supposing from your silences,
you told me I was wrong.

You need the charm of each C sharp
as China needs the secret music of growing rice.
Ideas with unreadable eyes hover over you in twos and threes,

choose you for their instrument, like Arab jinns
which perch on a man's shoulder and drive him till he drops.
They go to your head and feet; your hands beat like hearts.
  Then every night, as you lose count, you hear,
beneath the other sounds, continual music:
a nightingale sings his twenty-four separate songs,
a sea-man plays a bamboo flute, and a hundred women
chant to seed the clouds. They measure and remeasure
your happiness and sorrow. They quarrel like Mongolians
over where exactly in Mongolia
music was invented. They work out to the ends of dreams
which are that you can't have the dreams.
You aren't the theme of everything.

  I need your voice the way I need the temperate evenings
on the verandah, the weight and threat of happiness;
you'd rather not talk about loving each other.
You expect to overhear pedestrians say exquisite things.
  The Japanese government issues an edict of sorrow:
there will be no transformation of all matter.
You can count all your life, you'll never know
why notions of time involve weight and blood.
Five thousand marines sing "Row Your Boat."
Your life is in a minor key, more suspense than substance.
  I try with ten fingers to hear your heart, counting away
in your chest. When will you accustom yourself to night and day
and love them as they are, one after the other?
You'll never know how many songs you know:
songs that show you are still a novice at suffering
and can't be sung in public,
danceable music, the Ode to Joy,
songs that make you sing.

for Imre and Maria Horner

Wild for to Hold

It was still summer then
and the hummingbirds clung to the sky with their wings.
Lizards flashed by, their frills billowing,
and cats on tiptoe snatched at moths.
Every strange, half-seen, half-hiding creature
showed us the most overwhelming friendliness
then withdrew as if to have a secret laugh.
Cats know by how they're touched
you love them. Isn't that so? I see myself
in their typical greetings, their sidlings
and soft little jumps, the way they turn in circles
and rub their heads on your legs.
She-panthers swayed in seasonal delirium
past leopards with expressive tails.
I was contained in your breath then
and didn't wonder when I'd be again.

Everything resembled our first years.
Nature said, "I'm your mother. Love me."
A brown wolf served her faithfully.
Seas and skies made their exchanges
and animals in odd alliances
appeared on intricate estuary landscapes.
Every spot of land had its own species,
none without good reasons for themselves.
Soft black kangaroos leapt into space,
giraffes stood casually on either sides of cyclones,
and dragon hatchlings grew up in the trees of Indonesia.
All of us had equal spans of life
in breaths and heartbeats.

One of those days, I slipped you a taste
of the longing under my tongue.
At midnight, animals groaned like men and men like animals.
People, beasts and birds closed circles, had their moments.
You tried not to get attached to the wild;
you needed to be in the world. But what you neglected
came back in your dreams: half-wild, half-gentled things
signaling friendship with a bite not hard enough to hurt.
You rescued from oblivion
the mixed breeds of myths—griffins and minotaurs;
the long-lost elephant birds, dawn horses;
and long lines of the threatened, waiting with bent shoulders.
They sang like animals in fables to the rocking motion
of the universe, "I am not your huntress but your heart."
        Imagined into life without a purpose, and indispensable,
they reminded you of us. You studied the Great Dyings,
sea shifts, supernovae, examined with surprise and terror
the surprise and terror sealed on fossil faces.
Were you doing this for me? I thought you were.

        A stag sprays himself more male
for the little doe who spreads her scent on the breeze.
An elephant cuddles a rhinoceros; a rhinoceros,
an armadillo. Bodies of sleeping women lie closing
after childbirth, nursing the illusion of infinity
given by tenderness.
        I thought it was a terrible confusion
that made the tiger spread his dread to his nieces and nephews.
I brought you all that was soft in me.
Now I think it's on a perfect autumn afternoon
that life turns cruel. Do you still believe that every creature
has its replica at the bottom of the sea?

They see how we watch when they're ready to leave
and they're always ready to leave,
cat-footing forward with the fugitiveness of wild things
conscious of a refuge somewhere. We drive them
out of the mountains: flamingos older than the Andes,
bobbing bobcats, flocks of sheep, down the slopes
in desperate devotion, past trip wires, fences, mines,
practicing the natural deceptions that protect
their old souls and impenetrable hearts. They don't even
have each other. We drive them out
of the valley: they live on the sides
of the mountains. The whispering loudens to crying
to shouting to voices chaotically shrieking "Keep Out!"
We also have enemies. (Do we have each other?)
    We watch them execute the steps of the dance
in which their lives will fly before them and at the same time
die behind them. Elephants distribute the bones of elephants,
and whooping cranes play the air with their black feathers.
Can't you see in their eyes you aren't there anymore,
that all you can do is be glad you have somewhere to go back to?

    One of these days, the cat asleep in the laurel tree
will decide to come down the trunk on the tips of her claws.
White birds flying over black reflections
will slip past your face, slanting on the wind
above a landscape intense enough to hold the world together.
Maybe you'll be waiting for me there. I almost think so.
    Paradise was always full of animals,
and there were seasons
when everything was free to be
as green or gray or shimmering as it pleased.
Families have a way of growing into strangers.

Departed souls of animals gather in the baobabs;
winged insects vanish, the calcium in eggshells, then the birds.
Hold us. We're leaving.
Brother in suffering,
you with the goat on your shoulders, the lamb at your feet,
don't we have it in us to go on more beautifully?

About the author

ALANE ROLLINGS was born in Savannah, Georgia, and grew up in the South. She attended Bryn Mawr College and received a B.A. and an M.A. from the University of Chicago. She has taught at Loyola University and the University of Chicago. In 1986, she received an Illinois Arts Council grant for her work on *In Your Own Sweet Time*. Her first book, *Transparent Landscapes*, was a Writer's Choice Pushcart/NEA selection in 1985. She earlier worked as a rental agent in Chicago, as an assistant survey director of the National Opinion Research Center at the University of Chicago, and as producer of the university television show "Perspectives." She lives in Chicago with her husband, novelist Richard Stern.

About the book

In Your Own Sweet Time was composed in Plantin by Graphic Composition, Inc. of Athens, Georgia. The Plantin typeface is named for the 16th-century Antwerp printer Christophe Plantin, although it is not certain that Plantin actually used the type on which it is based. Plantin was designed by F. H. Pierpont, and introduced in the 1920s by the Monotype Corporation of England.

The design is by Kachergis Book Design, Inc. of Pittsboro, North Carolina.

WESLEYAN UNIVERSITY PRESS, 1989